Editors: Sarah Maclin, Doug Linert

Cover Design: Troy Miles

Illustrations: Troy Miles

Acknowledgements

To Dad: my Mentor and Idol.   To Mom: my "Beacon of Light."
To Xavier and Zarius: my greatest Joys. My desire to make you all proud is a pillar of strength.

To my Family and Friends: Your love and support has buoyed me through every period of my life.

Special Thanks to Coach Dee Hawkes for your wisdom and insight.

To all the other coaches, teammates, people and places that have indelibly left marks on my basketball soul: *Coach Ed Wilson*, Michael Miles, Mike McCrory, Lake Waterford, Civic Center, Green Hornets (Quentin Jackson, Cyrul Palmer (CP), Bobby Puera, Scotty Wilkins and Scotty Fox), Lenny Fontes, Danny Ferry, Howie Landa, All-Pro Camp- Sam Bowie, Campy Russell, Walker Russell, Terry Furlow, Benny White, Bernie Fine, Kevin Coughlin, Jim Gorman and Maurice Jennings, Charles Carter, Bruce Springer, Severna Park Junior High '77, "Doctor Dirt", Gary Ladd, Greg Williams, Damon Eaves, Greg Kalina, , "Doc" Brown, Michael Hall, Al Moyer, Jack Schalow, Connolly Center, NYSP, '78 Chieftains & Supersonics, Al Moyer, Keith Harrell, Clint Richardson, Carl Ervin, Tony Barnes, Terry Jones, John Jordan, Joe Buchanan, Keith Richardson, Craig Richardson, Joyce Walker, Terry Kinnebrew, Michael Simmons, Mark Struthers, Larry Brooks, Bernard Hill, Larry Martin, Gene McClanahan, Rob Silver, Bob Love, Peter Patitucci, Brian Brooks, Stan Mahan, Gary Schneider, Paine Field, IMA, Green Lake, Bobby Calhoun, '83 Irish, Darrin Levy, "Jumpin" Joe Asberry, Roman Miller, Jim Caviezel, Dan Raley, JoJo Rodriguez, David Barton, Dunk Kings '83, Big Orange Camp (Syracuse), Caldwater Park, N.J., St. Cecelia's (Detroit), Bobby Joe Hunter, UNR '84, Quentin Stephens, Uvonte Reed, Curtis High, Mercer County College '85- Jerald Wrightsil, Andre Britton, Ken Blaze, Ed Boone, Troy Stevens and family, Victor "Spontaneous" Alvin, Sonny Hill Summer League (Philadelphia), Nate Duchesne, Idaho State '86, Jim Boutin, Barry Janusch, George "Eddie" Davis, Chase Brown, Don Holston, Craig Murray, James Ferguson, Rotary, (Yes) Lou Hopson, Miles Ahead, Ron Mulberg, Phil Lumpkin, John Johnson, Linda Fisher, *John Wooden*, Red Auerbach, John Thompson, Al McGuire, Vince Lombardi, Lou Pinnella, Bill Russell, Naim Abdul-Aziz, Muhammad Ali, Bruce Lee, Edgar Martinez, Ichiro Suzuki, Willie Miller.

Along with basketball's great stars, illustrious history and unparalleled pageantry, you all have shared in and contributed to my love of the game.

Table of Contents

FOREWORD BY LENNY WILKENS IV

PASSION FRUITS V

INTRODUCTION 1

1   VIRTUAL PLAY 4

2   BRAIN GAME 8

3   EVALUATION FIXATION 13

4   WE CAN BUILD YOU 17

5   THE SIX F'S OF SHOOTING 23

6   CAN YOU HANDLE IT? 30

7   PASSING THE TEST 40

8   OBVIOUSLY OPEN 44

9   LANE PLAY 49

10 LINE DRIVE 54

11 BACKBOARD MASTERY 59

12 "D" OR DIE? 62

13 LANE PATROL 72

14 PROTECT THE QUEEN 75

15 "BOUND" TOGETHER 78

16 THE VIRTUAL ARTIST 81

Education = Acquisition

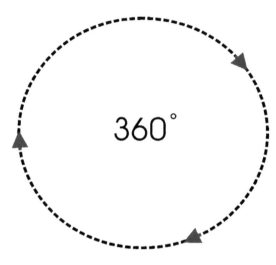

360°

Application = Performance

May this material be a new testament for a new millennium player

FOREWORD

It seems like yesterday when Troy was a young kid hanging around our practices during our championship season in Seattle. After reading the material in this book it's apparent that time has certainly moved forward. "The Virtual Game..." contains a wealth of knowledge that reflects years of experience and pedigree. I am a firm believer in basketball as model for success. The ingredients for success are the same in life as in basketball. I respect the energy and effort Troy has put forth to provide you with a legitimate opportunity to develop yourself as a player and individual.

Basketball is a game of maximizing advantages. It is to your advantage to allow the "The Virtual Game..." to help you. There's information inside these pages for players of all levels - including college and pro. It definitely holds everyone to a high standard of play. It's rooted in the fundamentals, yet provides esoteric material that will hold your interest and expand your thinking. I give this book a "thumbs up."

Lenny Wilkens - Former NBA Player and Coach

PASSION FRUITS

There is no Passion without Love. If it takes work to motivate you to work, are you sure you are in the right line of work? What is better than doing what you feel passionate about? It has been said that if you are working inside your passion sphere, you are not working at all. Passion is the fuel that helps you motor through the tedium of all that is required of you on your journey to where you want to go. Passion helps you keep your eye on the prize. It allows you to

The passage of time is an involuntary act that will continue to happen long after we have passed on. Change is a voluntary act that happens as a result of how we use our time.

manage the discomforts of change and facilitate growth. Passion grants the power to turn setbacks into stepping-stones and disappointments into road maps for future success. Passion bears fruits of labor and love, intertwined with discipline and dedication to details; which in the end, makes the taste so sweet. What is more rewarding than choosing a path, facing whatever challenge and finding success in it? Most people want to fulfill their dreams. If not for a little adversity, distraction and inaction, so many would. Success comes before Work only in the dictionary, but never comes before Passion.

Introduction

I humbly share Coach Brown's sentiments. I invite you on a journey to a basketball place where you might not have been before. Being well versed in the fundamentals is a great and necessary start for effective play. However, the addition of math and physics to your applications will move your game into a different realm. This book is an opportunity for you to become a more capable basketball person: physically, technically, intellectually and emotionally. No matter how well you play or what league you play in, this book will make you more refined in technique and sharper in application. The goal of my instruction is to help you to become machine-like across all of your basketball functions by creating default settings for consistent or automated performance.

The truth is the math and science of the game never changes when it comes to successful play. In fact, most successful players do the same things. Oftentimes these players are not aware of or even concerned with the mathematical or scientific realities of their actions. They have success doing what they do, so they continue to do it. Unfortunately, most players are not so lucky. Think about it. What are the chances of randomly acquiring the necessary skill sets to become a top player? As a result, "stars" are rare. That means most players are in desperate need of the right information or materials to become the diamond of their dreams.

But how do you get there without knowing what you do not know or, worse, not knowing you do not know? What is needed is some sort of guide to help you down the path. The guide could be an individual, reference material or both. The key element is you must thirst for the knowledge and then see the value of working to apply it. Most players just want to go play, which leads us to why diamonds are such a rare occurrence. Playing is important, but only a part of the developmental equation. Diamonds and top-level performers are products of **MPT:** the right **M**aterials, proper **P**ressure and ample **T**ime for it all to come together. In basketball terms, **MPT** equates to: quality coaching and application, challenging competition, and consistent dedication to personal development.

Exposure to the right materials is critical. This is why Virtual Play can take you a quantum leap forward with your game. It represents the basketball matrix, where all elements necessary for maximum outcomes are broken down into digestible parts for you to download or **program** into your system. Focusing on optimizing every function will boost your performance dramatically.

Virtual Play is the martial arts of basketball. It is the fundamentals, centered on economy and strategy of movement. With Virtual Play you do not have to be the best athlete to be the best player. The only physical requirement is to be an average athlete - if that. With superior technique, you can control physical confrontations without dependency on raw force or speed. Virtual Play allows you to manipulate time and space to manage objects beyond your "normal" physical capacity. Just like in the first *Matrix* movie (watch it if you get a chance), Neo did not change the speed of the bullets. Instead, he used strategy and economy of movement to manipulate physical circumstances to create an illusion of tremendous speed for the viewer and, most importantly, to escape injury.

It is precision of technique and focused vision that allows you to slow the game speed down to make processing the action easier. Precision or "clean" technique eliminates unnecessary movements and other time-costs from your play. Focused vision (which provides early awareness of the immediate circumstance) speeds up anticipation and decision-making skills. This type of time efficiency allows you to operate ahead of the action without having to move fast physically.

In the end, you are the sum of your skills plus your confidence and courage to put them on display. You must face the challenging process of self-development and skill implementation. It requires you to find a way to truly believe in yourself and all that you have put into your system. This book is a tool to help you see it, believe it and ultimately achieve it. Usually when we create a deep enough belief in something, we then have the power to get things done. I hope you find value on these pages to move you forward. They are filled with **Information, Demonstration, Explanation and Verification**, that what I am offering is a truth. Not the only truth, but a layered and fundamentally sound model for consistent success. I encourage you to read on. I guarantee that this material will help sharpen the most valuable tool in your arsenal: You!

1
VIRTUAL PLAY

There is a tremendous amount of information out there about basketball. The library covers almost every topic. Over the past 100+ years, basketball has done its share of changing. There have been several rule changes; players and teams have changed; and of course, the peripherals of the game are ever changing. Despite an ever-evolving game with high flying and "and-1" moves in the mix, the basic blue print for success has remained relatively the same. Dr. Naismith would be proud of that. Could

You have arrived as a Virtual Player when your basketball success is based on your ability to apply the fundamentals of Basketball, Mathematics, and Physical Science as a single discipline.

Dr. Naismith fathom the above-the-rim acrobatics or street-ball creativity of the modern player? This era of the physical freak has morphed the game of basketball beyond physical recognition. It is becoming more and more difficult to compete on today's athletic plane. The odds of being the most physically gifted player on the court are quite slim. Even if you are today, you may not be tomorrow. For sustained success you must continue to grow in your knowledge (**Know-How**) of the game and continue to sharpen your application of technique. Fortunately, in the world of Virtual Play, the measure of performance is determined by the net results of actions and not necessarily the physical prowess of the performer. Would it matter whether you are more physical than me, if I am continually going past you or controlling you? In this scenario, the net result would be the same: you being physically superior, and me, continually running past or manipulating you to my advantage.

Moreover, the ability to manipulate time, space and opponents beyond the use of just basketball fundamentals is the trademark of a Virtual Player (VP). VP's understand the math and science of the game. This application bridges the gap between the super-freak and the average athlete. Mathematics is the body of knowledge that studies such concepts as structure, quantity, space and change. It also explores concepts and establishes truths with rigorous deduction. In this book, I will present to you some of the concepts you must master to become technically competent as a VP, able to transfer those concepts effectively at any level of physical play. Do not let yourself feel confused at this point. The information will all make more sense as you read on.

Physics, in one form or another is one of the oldest academic disciplines. It seeks to understand very basic concepts such as force, mass, energy and momentum. Through the use of precise movement i.e. explosive starts, stops and effective use of angles to create leverage and directionality, you will be able to execute in ways that will produce matrix-like outcomes during play. You will become a basketball optical illusion - the Neo of the hardwood. In fact, you will be your fastest and most manipulative in your shortest steps relative to the opposition. Because this methodology actually requires less physical effort, it will allow you to operate with greater physical control of yourself and the game circumstance. It is a powerful feeling.

Imagine Bruce Lee. He would fight a host of worthy adversaries throughout his movies, only to get to the old man at the end. The old man was never the most physically gifted, yet posed Bruce's stiffest challenge. He performed far beyond his physical stature with expert timing (mathematical precision of movement) and other abilities reflecting his experience or

Know-How. Martial art has shown for centuries that there are no mathematical or physical limits to optimizing technique or execution. Therefore, there is no limit to improving, right? So regardless of how well you play, how athletic you are or how much you know, there is always room to increase your proficiency and performance.

The power lies in ultimate focus on applying the basics as an art form. It makes athleticism less of a factor. It allows you to transcend physical deficiencies - if there are any - and negate the physicality of our opponents. Net speed, quickness and strength are a matter of superior preparation to respond (timing) and superior application of technique. This, of course, is rooted in the fundamentals of whatever sport.

Virtual Play, as you will discover, is the technical and physical model for optimum efficiency in basketball. The more precise you are in applying these principals the more effective you are in your play. Of course, there will always be guys who have success off of what they can do physically or by way of trickery. These players operate on **Do-How** as opposed to Know-How. They are highly capable and often physical freaks of some sort. Too often however, their inadequate comprehension or application of fundamentals limits their chance for consistent success. Know-How will win the series against Do-How almost always. Now of course, Know-How combined with Do-How...that would be "Jordanian."

Hopefully you are beginning to understand Virtual Play conceptually. Let us look at how it works actually. Basketball is one of the few sports in which the offense has the advantage. Unfortunately, many players and teams give theirs away with poor technique and a flawed offensive approach. One of the keys to offensive manipulation is the right to move first. This **law of leadership** gives the offensive player the ability to deceive or control opponents with intentions or false intentions to go places or do things. If all of our movements are in frames - as in motion pictures - and we can learn to control our movement in each frame, then we should then be able to mislead and manipulate opponents with our intentions in early frames of movement. It is extremely difficult to predict anyone's start, stoppage or change of movement. Furthermore, the defender must match the rate of the proposed movement in those early frames or risk being moved past. Therefore, we can control our opponents by proposing an action and being continuously contrary to their responses. And given the typical controlled rate of a Virtual Player's movement, it becomes easy to make necessary changes to exploit or maintain advantage. This will be explained in greater detail in chapter 5, "Can you Handle It".

The discovery of optimization in Virtual Play has been absolutely fascinating and it never stops. Uncovering these truths and absolutes is the portal to peak performance in many endeavors, especially sports. Technology will forever change. You must adapt to these changes or be prepared to fall short of your objectives. As in *The Matrix*, the challenge for you now is deciding which "pill" to take: Do you read on now, or do you put the book down and go back to your old basketball life?

2
BRAIN GAME

Did you know that you are not your brain? Your brain is a programmable instrument over which you have dominion. Our involuntary functions - like heartbeat and breath, are programmed by God, Nature, the Universe, or whatever creative force you believe in. Our Voluntary functions - how we perform or do things is programmed by our physical and mental experiences.

Think about this: the most vital life source is your breath, yet you can have power over it by interjecting a command to your brain to hold your breath. This is an act of exercising dominion over your body. As a human you are a remarkable creature. You have the capacity to do unbelievable things. What you need to do is convince your brain that what you want to achieve is possible. In order to believe, you have to envision it or experience it. I am not yet another person giving you my opinions about basketball – we know the world is full of those. Rather, I will help you understand all the phases of skill acquisition with verifiable information based on experimentation.

Many of us have seen the movie *The Matrix.* As I mentioned earlier, this film will help you understand programming or skill acquisition as it relates to Virtual Play. In the movie, acquisition was a matter of plugging into the chair and having information downloaded directly into the brain. The information downloaded was designed for optimal performance. No sense in downloading garbage, right? Programming in Virtual Play is very similar, only there is no chair and you are required to download the information manually - repetition by repetition. In my experience I have found it may take up to ten thousand positive reps to fully integrate or program a function into your system. It is even more painstaking to overwrite or change an existing function or habit. You must continually interject commands to your brain to make it perform in a particular manner until it is fully automated.

If you can understand how to perform a function, then you have the power to program it into our brain. You can train your brain for gain in the direction you choose. It is a struggle at first. The brain fights hard to hold onto the established function (old program). Its first line of defense is to attack your emotions, upset you, or prompt your negative self-talk - whatever way it can manage to derail or delay any changes: "I'm tired", "This is stupid", or "I can't do this." Maybe you have heard one of these? It takes courage and hard work to make changes to your system. I tell players all the time not to be discouraged by the discomfort of change - particularly if it is a change for the better.

You can expedite change by doing both physical and mental reps. **Mental-repetition** is the process of visualizing performance without physically doing the function. You can sit in a chair with your eyes closed and watch yourself perform **positive** or clean reps. Mental-reps will actually improve your technique. They may not be as powerful as physical reps, but five mental reps may equal one physical rep. However you slice it, it still equates to a lot of hard work on the right materials. Every rep you perform counts. Negative training is more common than one might think. You are either moving in a positive direction toward perfection or a negative one towards a world of higher degree of difficulty. So make sure the information you are dealing with is valid and that each rep is as *clean* as possible.

Diagram 2A

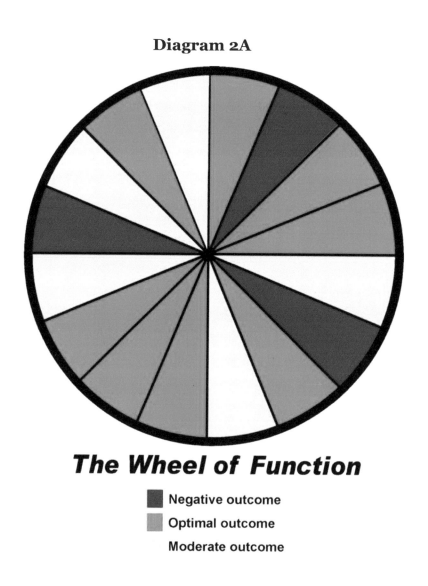

The Wheel of Function

■ Negative outcome
■ Optimal outcome
Moderate outcome

The television game show "The Wheel of Fortune" outlines the principles of **programming**. On the show, the slots on the wheel are full of dollar amounts and prizes. The contestants spin the wheel and it lands on a certain slot. It rarely lands on the same slot more than once, but it always lands on a slot. Your brain, similarly, is **"The Wheel of Function"** (Diagram 2A) with slots full of programmed information of how you perform or do certain things. When you are called to action - to shoot a basketball or execute a dribble maneuver - your brain spins and it lands on one of the programmed slots for performance. In this case you would typically shoot exactly according to your existing script. With enough positive repetition your technical wheel for shooting can be filled with slots of the optimal way to perform (Diagram 2B).

Diagram 2B

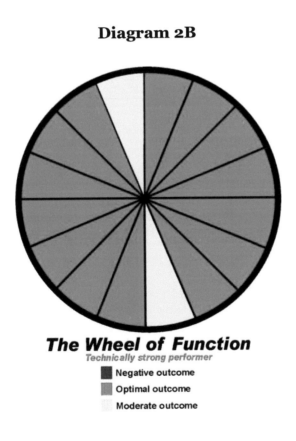

The Wheel of Function
Technically strong performer

■ Negative outcome
■ Optimal outcome
Moderate outcome

It is a tough task to make changes to your system. But once change is programmed in, however the struggle, it will be just as difficult for your brain to operate outside of the "new" programmed material. Automation grants independence of mind-space and breeds confidence. Still, you must believe that you will be able to perform regardless of the environment or pressure of the moment. This level of confidence and **swag** does not come cheap. You must invest in yourself whole-heartedly. It will cost you literally thousands of positive repetitions to create the proper defaults and emotional resolve for consistent quality performances. The bottom line: you must pay to play in a special way. Everyone wants to, but who actually gets to?

3
EVALUATION FIXATION

**The best coaches focus on player development
as opposed to player replacement**

It is a tough task to evaluate players. It is even more difficult to evaluate yourself. There are so many factors the process can become complex quickly. Below is a system I have used to help determine the **proficiency** and **efficiency** of any given player. Proficiency denotes absolute skill value and efficiency concerns effectiveness of skill use during play. This system has been a valuable tool in helping me differentiate top players from the crowd. It has also been useful in helping players gain a truer sense of self, particularly to understand areas of concern for their development.

Evaluations are twofold: (1) Rating players according to defined roles as an **Efficiency Rating (ER)**; and (2) Rating players according to their capability - **PTAG** (below).

PTAG

(1) Physical ability, (2) Technical acuity

(3) Intellectual Application of # (1) and #(2)

(4) Heart and Grit.

Physical talent is great but it is nothing without technical skill. Technical skill is great if properly applied. However, heart and grit are the soul of any player. Some players just have that "thing": it is hard to put a finger on or define it, yet it is so easy to recognize. Many times grit is the deciding factor between otherwise equal adversaries. In fact, a high **Grit-factor** raises the other three categories up a notch. Without it you may lose confidence under adversity, experience diminished skills or even the capacity to think clearly.

Everyone at some point has succumbed to pressure and performed poorly. It does not necessarily make you heartless - just human. Coaches tell players to be tough all the time. But what is tough really? What is "hard-nosed"? There are a number of factors that contribute to toughness and fortitude. Attitude and physical prowess are often key components, but grittiness - the ability to **hyper-focus** 100% on what is necessary for success in each moment of exchange - might be the most important. As a coach, I demand intensity and intelligence from players, but above all focus. Thankfully this can be manufactured and developed.

Focus = grittiness = toughness

Maybe you are not built to be rough and tumble, but you can learn to hyper-focus. Obviously this type of focus is difficult to come by. The mind is susceptible to distraction. Still, I push players to observe the **10 to 7** rule as a way to find emotional calm inside the tension of the moment: Get hyped and focused on level 10; accept all the emotions of the moment; then take a deep breath and calm your mind to 7 for play. A colleague of mine says, "What is required in the fray is a **Calm Assertive Mind.** It allows you to operate in a state that enables you to process the action and function at the same time."

14

Even though humans are the greatest machines on earth, you are still responsible for managing your emotions. Maintaining composure under trying circumstances is an extreme challenge. The good news is you can systematically increase your grit or **G-factor** to make yourself environment proof. It is not hocus pocus, but rather continuous focus...on the right things.

The second phase of evaluations - **ER** - attaches a numerical value to a player's effectiveness inside a given role. Players typically have primary and secondary roles. Upper case letters denote primary roles (i.e. **SC**); lower case denotes secondary roles (i.e. **sc**). I rate players in each area 1 to 5; with 5 being the highest level. Role classification and symbols will vary from coach to coach. Exhibit A below is my personal list of role definitions.

SC differs from **S** in terms of how a player scores. **S** refers mainly to spot-up shooters and **SC** for players that score in different ways inside the offense. **P** describes an assist person - any position. **D** refers to on–ball defenders and shot blockers. **MM** or "momentum man" defines a big play person who impacts the game without scoring necessarily: key steal, block, charge, etc. **PM** refers to an individual who spearheads the fast break.

Evaluations include a brief overview **(OV)** or blueprint for continuous improvement, along with identification of core strengths. A few examples follow below. (Note: evaluations can be done according to any timetable or schedule.)

For scouting purposes: this system has kept me on task in identifying players and their core abilities without regard to the hoopla surrounding them or how they might have played (technically) on that particular occasion.

Examples

Player: #1- Harris

> **Role:** PM-P-D-MM

> **ER:** 3-4-5-1

> **PTAG:** 5-3-3-5

> **OV:** Improve shooting proficiency and efficiency, plus control negative emotionality

> **Core strength**: Leadership qualities and ability to compete

Player: #7- Davis

> **Role:** SC-S-R-P

> **ER:** 3-2-4-2

> **PTAG:** 3-4-3-3

> **OV:** Must improve resolve, ability to lead by example and improve positive self-talk

> **Core strength:** Technical skill sets and "go-to" capability

4
We can build you

The goal is to become machine-like (in efficiency) across all basketball functions.

One NBA player calls himself "The Machine." He believes his shooting technique and proficiency is machine-like in action and result. The shooting mechanics of a machine are based on mathematical construction and scientific function for maximum efficiency. How do 45° and 90° angles aid in this measure? Do you have the right tools to be machine-like in your overall basketball play?

Your body is the greatest tool at your disposal. You must learn to use it for maximum net physical outcomes. Your physical ability is an important element and I encourage you to work diligently to enhance it. Still, the concern of this section is less about your physical **capacity** (what you have) and more about your physical **capability** (what you do with what you have). You can accomplish a lot physically with technical precision instead of brawn.

Diagram 4A

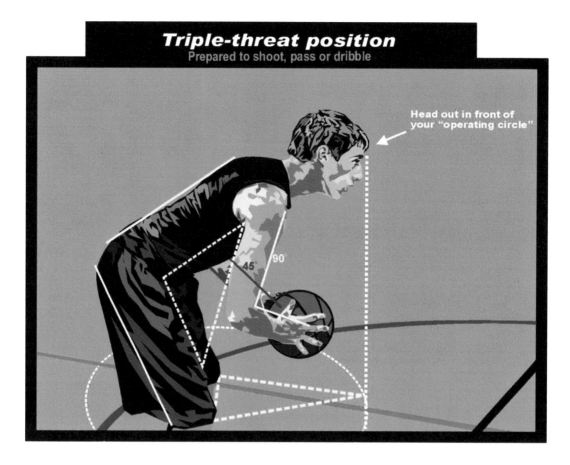

Let us talk about **structure:** In triple threat position the tip of the head should create a triangle with the feet (Diagram 4A). This is the athletic position for many sports. Now imagine that you are a vehicle (Diagram 4B). Your feet are the wheels and the head and shoulders are the steering column. The outer shoulders, torso and arms make up the body of the unit. And as a vehicle you should lead with your head and shoulders. It is similar to a running back headed downfield. The head, shoulders and torso area help protect the ball as you move toward triple threat or **structure**. This area between the feet out to the head is known as the **operating circle** or

cage area. The cage is your personal operating space and serves as a safe haven for the basketball under duress. No one should be able to enter that space without fouling you or allowing you to get past them.

Diagram 4B

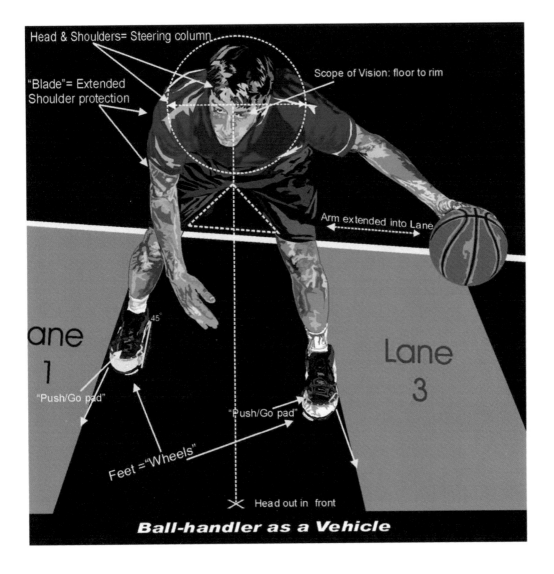

The base of a vehicle would be the axle or, in basketball terms, your stance. Stance is the distance between the feet. It is very important to maintain this space at all times on the floor. The basic fundamental is feet should be kept at shoulders-length apart. However, a slightly wider stance gives you superior balance and greater absolute (net) speed. Absolute speed is about being on both sides of the line or in two places at the same time. A wider stance also increases your "sphere of influence" or operating circle.

Diagram 4C

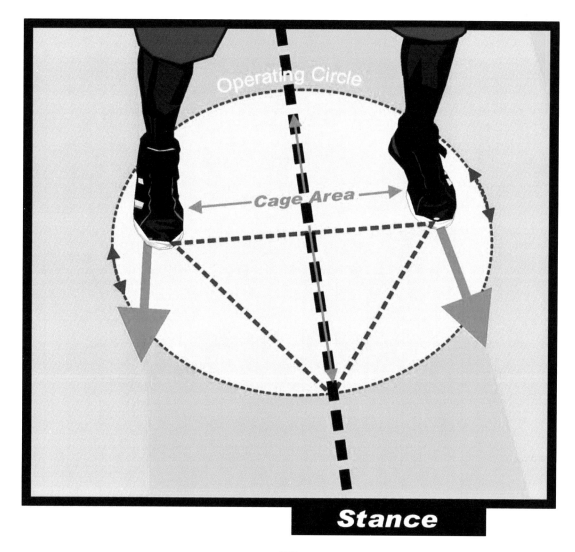

A quality player always maintains stance and makes use of the **total cage area** or circumference of his operating circle. Be careful not to compromise your stance while pivoting. The base is too important. Make sure you use your thighs to push energy out over your feet to maintain your **pyramid** (between the thighs). With a solid base, all your parts can work together in a hydraulic fashion to makes explosive movement more economical. Without proper structure your athletic outcome is compromised and your response time to act is also diminished.

Most effective ballplayers understand how to be **"spinning tops"** or **pivot machines**. Up top, sound pivoting involves shoulder protection and chin movements shoulder-to-shoulder for quicker vision and awareness. Shoulder-to-shoulder with the chin uses the diameter of the circle to cut unnecessary frames and speed up vision awareness of others. Down below: use of the inside foot to pivot and **push** and the outside foot to stabilize. The outside or **control foot**, like the jab of the boxer, keeps defenders at bay with threats to punch or - in the case of basketball threats - to spin or go by. Going by the defender is actually establishing the push foot and pivoting past with the control foot. Just like the chin shoulder-to-shoulder action, the control is a 180-degree spin (pivot) forward, making use of the diameter of the circle.

Proper footwork in basketball is as vital to successful play as effective skating is to quality hockey play. After all, foot control (explosive stops and starts) is a key element of body control and controlling opponents. If you cannot skate, you will never be an effective hockey player regardless of your other skills; likewise in basketball. Therefore you must understand how your feet operate. The feet are made of two parts. The balls of the feet are the **Go** or **Push pads** and are used to power your system. The heels are the

brakes and are used primarily for stopping and stabilization. Having your energy backward on your heels or operating on the brakes means you are stuck (flat) to the floor and slower to react. (Note: Engaging the toes to the floor in a gripping fashion shifts your energy forward and keeps you on your pads. This promotes instant forward movement or explosion. We will revisit this later in "Can You Handle it?")

Power to mobilize or power to perform any other basketball function is generated with the feet and transferred through the butt and up the body for specific use. The next chapter will show you how to use that power and operate as a shooting machine.

5

The Six F's of Shooting

Shooting proficiency is based on how well you shoot the ball technically. Shooting efficiency is the net of shooting proficiency and game time factors such as shot selection.   Diagram 5A

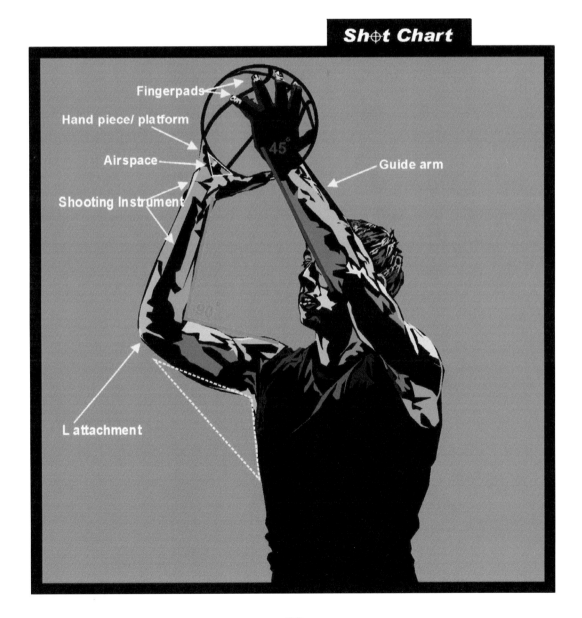

The name of the game literally is basketball. The name of the game figuratively is putting the ball in the basket. This is known as the art of shooting. At the end of the game, the team with the most baskets (points) is the winning team. That sounds simple enough. If only getting the ball in the basket was as easy. Shooting and the positive result – scoring - are arguably the most important parts of the game. Even if you hold your opponent scoreless with great defense, you still must score at least once to win. The ability to shoot the ball well is a great asset for an individual and team. A good shooter commands space (between catch-spot and the basket) and thereby expands defensive coverage area. This not only affords more opportunities to score but also greater freedom to negotiate and be productive in other offensive ways.

How does a person become a great shooter? Do all the best shooters shoot the same way? Do you have to be a natural or can anyone learn the basics and become a quality shooter?

Like any skill acquisition, shot development requires consistent positive programming. Not everyone shoots exactly the same way, nor is it necessary - although there are some non-negotiable elements that make it easier to shoot effectively. It is true that not all good shooters have sound technique. There are a number of unorthodox shooters who shoot quite well. In the end, all quality shooter's shots travel towards the basket with enough height and distance for the ball to find its way through the cylinder, which is ultimately dictated by the follow through of the **control finger** toward the target (**Diagram 5B**). However they do it, good shooters typically shoot the same way each time they attempt a shot. Develop a style that is as close to the fundamentals as possible, yet comfortable given your particular physical make-up. After all, the most critical element is the

finish or **follow-through.** The follow-through is your radar system to the basket.

Diagram 5B

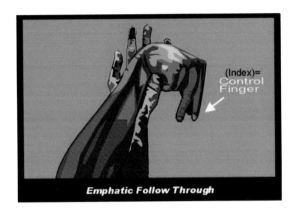

Emphatic Follow Through

Did you know two men's and more than two women's basketballs fit into the hoop at once? Still the best game-time shooters shoot about fifty percent. Therefore, it is important to work hard to give yourself the best opportunity to make each shot. First, consider if you are capable of making the shot from that area consistently. Second, consider whether it is the best shot for the team (at that moment) or if it is even necessary to shoot. Continue to learn the game intellectually to become a better decision-maker about when to shoot or from where to shoot.

When it comes to the mechanics of shooting, people teach different things and methods vary. Since Virtual Play's aim is to become machine-like in your approach, let us suppose that you are a well-crafted shooting machine made of four basic parts: (1) feet: **Thrusters;** (2) legs and torso: **Main Beam;** (3) arm at 90°: **L attachment;** (4) hand-piece or fingertips: **Platform.** The thrusters or push-pads are the base of the machine and the source for power as we talked about in the last chapter. Think of thrusters powering rockets into space with the power starting at the base. The common fundamental says use your legs for power. This is true to an extent. Focus more specifically on exploding or pushing your feet, especially if your shot is a little off. Start with your feet to make adjustments.

The **Main Beam** is vital to the proper transfer of that power from the feet through the fingertips. In basketball, the fingertip is defined as the area from the top of the finger to the first knuckle. Together the hand-piece and L attachment make up the shooting **"instrument"** (**Diagram 5A**).

*(**Power transfer tip**: For free-throw attempts or set shots, the ball should be released from the fingertips before the legs straighten. For jump shots, use your arms to help elevate higher and release the ball up and out (towards the front rim) at the top of the jump.)*

On the **Hand-piece**, the fingertips provide the platform for the ball to rest on (Diagram 5 B). It is important that the ball start here as opposed to the palm or flat against the entire finger. The fingertips provide better control of the ball, and that is proven every time you attempt to *palm* the ball. You palm and flat-fingered shooters, ask yourself: am I settling for less than optimal control for shooting? I will bet you cannot palm the ball with your entire hand touching it. You should program into your delivery as much fingertip control as possible. Further, the director of the platform is the index or **control finger**. It is the only finger that points directly at the target. Try it. As you point at the target, the other fingers all angle away from the target. The control finger ultimately determines the path the ball will travel with the least degree of difficulty. It should be the last finger to make contact with the ball as part of an emphatic finish at the target.

Diagram 5C

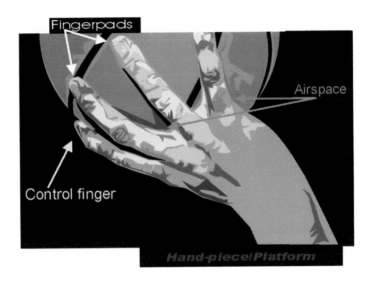

MATH TASK: If you are facing the basket, the main beam (your legs and torso) should be perpendicular to the floor and your shoulders parallel to the backboard. The L attachment connects to the main beam forming a ninety-degree angle and the ball rests on the concave platform created the fingertips and hand-piece. The **"fifth" piece** or **guide arm** attaches to the ball at 45° (**diagram 5 A**). You are now ready for use. Since every machine has a proper functionality it is important to operate inside that framework.

This chapter outlines the most efficient way to operate as a shooting machine. The *6F's* will serve as a checklist of sorts to help in the programming process. The F's are broken down into two sets of three: **Preparing to shoot: Feet, Forward** and **Frozen; and Preparing to make the shot: Front rim** (target), **Feet over** (how high above the rim or aim); and of course, **Follow through to Finish**.

Here are the **6F's** in more detail:

(1) Feet: Your feet are your source for power and your main contact with the floor. Make sure you have a solid base and push with your feet. Creating energy with your feet is different than just bending our knees. Your knees should be unlocked and will bend naturally as you initiate power using your feet, thighs and butt. That power can be transferred from the feet through to the fingertips as long as your energy is moving... **(2) Forward** from triple threat position, with your butt moving outward to collect the energy. An inward-moving butt will stop the flow of energy just as crimping a water hose will stop the flow of water. In such a case the shooter will be forced to generate energy with the arms, which invariably leads to a throw or catapult. Our history books have shown us the use of the catapult. Should any of us be interested in having such a delivery?

(3) Frozen implies that the shooter has squared his feet and shoulders to the basket and ideally, will remain that way through the finish. If squared, the shooter should be able to walk forward and end up directly under the basket. Not only does this provide the mathematically "cleanest" opportunity to make shots, it is also the cleanest means to slip past a lunging defender under control. This gets you to the next spot on the path to the basket quickly without having to move fast physically.

(4) Front rim should be the shooting target. I have known or heard of very few fantastic shooters whose target was the back rim or the basket area in general. Back rim shooters are identifiable by the nature of their misses: clanks off the back iron. Golfers do not aim to shoot past the cup. It is likely where the ball would go. Even if the ball was online to the cup, it would not be soft enough or in the case of a basketball have enough touch (softness) to go into the hole.

During the second phase of the machine drill, the requirement is to hit the front rim from **(5) (two) Feet over**, with proper **(6) Follow through to Finish** - without making it. This is difficult to do. It is a low probability that the ball will actually hit the narrow front rim. Over time you will develop control enough to be able hit the rim mostly and even have the ball come back to your hand. However, what will generally happen is the ball- even against your wishes - will go into the basket. If by trying to hit the front rim only, the ball goes into the basket continually; should the front rim be the logical target? Changing the probability around can also help take pressure off trying to make shots. Square up, power from your feet, aim two feet over the front rim with an emphatic follow through and expect the shot to go in.

The 6 F's are for programming purposes only. During actual play, the focus should scale down to **Feet** (for power) and **Follow through to Finish.** However, the **6F's** do give the shooter an opportunity to self-correct on every attempt if necessary. **F** violations can be identified and adjustments can be made every attempt, even on makes. For example, if I shot the ball without arch or height, I would remind myself, "Feet over" to raise the level of the ball. If the ball travels off line, it could be an issue of follow through at the target. If shot correctly, adhering to the principles of the 6F's and machine shooting, the ball should enter the basket and return to your shooting hand. The ball typically filters out of the basket directly opposite the way it enters.

6

Can You Handle it?

Footwork + Bodywork + Dribbling = Ball handling

Ball handling + Scope of vision = Handling opponents

Dribbling is about controlling the basketball. The dribble is an essential element of play. It takes you where you need to go on the court in a legal way. Dribbling starts with the hand and involves how the fingers attach to the ball. It is easier to control the ball with the fingertips and the hand arched to match the concavity of the ball. This promotes pushing and following through instead of slapping at the ball. *Handles in a Hurry* at the end of the chapter outlines a series of dribble drills that will help develop ball and foot control.

The idea is to be vehicle-like in your approach to handling, or transporting, the ball. That would make your feet the wheels and brakes, and your head and shoulders the steering column. Of course, you are always the designated driver responsible for navigating the course. Therefore, proper **scope of vision** is a must. Proper scope of vision starts with eyes at rim level; which enables a broader vision area. In this scenario, the defender is the rider. Basketball grants the offensive player the **Law of leadership** or the right to be first. (You will read this as **position "A"** in the Chapter on "Lane Play".) This keeps the defender ... on the defensive. As with any vehicle, when you move forward (press the gas), the rider moves (falls) back. When you stop (hit the brakes) the rider moves forward. When you have the ball you possess similar control of a driver. Watching the opponent from the feet up gives early information about defensive intentions. It also allows you to see teammates and other defenders readily.

Focus on traveling in a straight line from wherever you are on the floor, with head, shoulders, and feet moving in the same direction *"on the road"* to the basket. It is not only the quickest route (between A and B) but it also provides the greatest threat to go by a defender. Maintaining a "threat to go by" is one of the keys to keeping the defender at bay and under your command. In the open-court (**freeway***),* dribbling waist high allows you to advance the ball effectively. Many dribblers cross the ball over from dribble lane to dribble lane. This is comfortable and allows the ball to cross through the triple-threat area for quick access to other options.

Dribbling above the ankle and below the knee provides greater control and protection in traffic. With your dribble arm by your side at 90° the starting point for your dribble is outside your foot towards the perimeter of your operating circle. It is important to protect the ball with your non-dribble arm extended over at 45° toward the ball. This juts out the shoulder and gives you maximum protection of the ball, plus it keeps your hands close for easier ball transition.

Fantastic dribblers are not necessarily quality ball handlers. **Dribblers-only** (dribbling without quality footwork or bodywork) can be magician-like in their ability to control the ball, yet far less talented at controlling the defender – especially within a dribble count or within proper spacing to stay connected with teammates in a productive manner. **Over-dribblers,** as many non-ball handlers are, delay fast-break opportunities and disrupt offensive continuity in the half-court. The goal should be to dribble when necessary and with purpose. Purposeful dribbling includes minimizing your dribbles between points A and B and maximizes each dribble in terms of space coverage. You can cover a lot of territory without many dribbles - particularly on drives to the basket.

Diagram 6A

Ball handling is the ability to dribble the ball, and to control your feet and body to execute options on the floor. Your feet get you where you need to go and proper body use solidifies whatever position you have gained on the floor. Without that type of control there is no true control, particularly of the operation speed to maintain or to gain advantage. This section will deal with learning to threaten (to go by) and manipulate opponents with proper foot and body management in lieu of speed.

Foot management starts with a wide stance. This provides stability and **absolute speed** (see: *Structure*, in Chapter 4). Absolute speed is being on both sides of the line or opponent at once. Maintaining stance makes changing side to side (right, left) or lane to lane as instantaneous as transferring the ball over. Pay attention to the stances of speedy and shifty players - in any sport.

Next is foot control. **Foot control** is the ability to negotiate **fractions of a step** versus just taking whole steps. If a whole step represents ten **frames** of movement, being able to stop in any frame - or at any point of movement toward a whole step, gives you control over individuals taking whole steps. Your opponent will have a difficult time predicting your starts and tops. This is where being fastest and most manipulative in your shortest steps comes into play. Defenders are required to take whole steps to defend threatened territory. It is of extreme importance to be aware of the **"Battle of the Feet."** Taking big steps only- as many players do, will make it more difficult for you to elude defensive cover- particularly if your opponent is more physically gifted. Foot and body control allow you to preserve your law of leadership by being continuously contrary to the responses of your opponent. This is the key to effective improvisation. In fact, forcing your opponent to act, then being contrary, allows you to stay ahead of the play.

Body control is about **changing levels** or bending the torso toward your center or structure with the head and shoulders out in front of your operating circle. **Changing levels, foot preparation** (for instant forward movement), and **arm extension** (to the perimeter of the cage), creates **range of motion.** Range of motion is very threatening to defensive security. It represents the early frames of movement to go by the defender and forces a defensive response in that direction at whatever speed is implied. That is the defender must match the implied speed of the early frames or risk a breech to the basket. This extension or threat whether drawn out (**slurred**) or short, allows your push foot to stay put and forces the defender to move over into another lane to cover the threat of your control foot. Now the defender is highly susceptible to a contrary forward movement and dominating bodywork regardless of his size or strength.

Bodywork is the negotiation of the space between the offensive and defensive players. It is to your advantage to move towards the defensive player with your **blade** (shoulder) and flex as quickly as possible without compromising your directionality towards the basket. Whoever dominates that space typically has the upper hand. This act is known as the **battle of the inner space**. The defender's job is to guard at arms length to stay ahead of the offensive player relative to the basket, in order to thwart penetration. Therefore, threatening to get your shoulder on her is essentially threatening to go by her. Once there is a breach and your blade is engaged, flexing and pushing towards the defender gives you leverage to maintain your position. Think about leaning against a door to prevent someone from barging in. It is a quick flex and steady push to hold your position. In this fashion, you can control the defender and continue on your journey without having to go fast. This keeps you prepared for any necessary change or quick stops. This will also allow you to process "reads" more judiciously and execute plays with greater ease. After all, this is how you "*handle* business."

Below is a series of drills designed to improve ball-handling.

Handle in a Hurry

All drills are done with the proper scope of vision.

Ball Squeeze

Rotate and squeeze the ball continuously while focusing on the fingertips and forearms.

(Key point: Squeeze as if trying to palm and pop it. Continue until the forearms and hands burn unbearably. Try to go deep into the burn.)

Power Dribbles

Rapid-fire dribbles below the knees and above the ankles, as fast as possible. Try to go deep into the burn.

(Key point: Focus on following extreme through with the fingertips.)

Pit-a-Pat

Three power dribbles followed by a swift crossover dribble to the other hand. Repeat.

(Key point: Focus on forward range of motion without turning the shoulders side-to-side, and extending the arm out into the lane before the cross back into the other lane. Keep hands close together. The movement should resemble the arm of a pendulum.)

Diamond Dribbles

A continuous dribble drill from front cross to diagonal cross between the legs dribble; then to a back cross, then to diagonal cross- back to front.

(Key point: Do odd-number changes. Do not over bend your knees; change levels instead. Establish a push foot and control foot to make sure you are prepared to move forward each exchange.)

Scissor Dribble

High speed, continuous, between the leg dribbles: right to left, left to right- feet back and forth.

(Key point: Continuous hover with extended arm range-of-motion at 90 $^{\circ}$ to 45°, then between-the-leg dribble. Try not to turn your shoulders. Try to control feet from moving too far.)

Dribble patrol

Dribble one front-crossover out to perimeter of cage, then a back-crossover to the other side. Repeat. It develops range of motion.

(Key point: Exhaust entire arm range of motion. At that point, the ball should be able to be crossed to the front or back.)

Push Drills

Push (explosion foot)/ Control foot

Propel yourself forward with the push foot and stop with the control foot. The **push foot** is typically the inside foot and opposite the ball. The **control foot** is typically the ball-side foot. Learn to paw with it in a way similar to the jab of a boxer in order to threaten to stride past the defender. Practice pushing and stopping your feet as you move up the floor. Change feet around for the return.

(Key point: establish a **push foot**-angled at 45° off the floor instead of keeping it flat and having it roll up to the toe. An angled push foot provides instant explosion, while a flat foot destroys your balance during range-of-motion.)

Diagram 6B

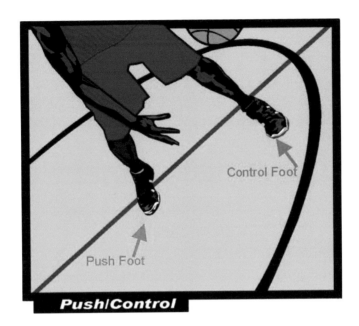

Change Sequences

(1) Quarter-step (for a direction change), (2) half-step to pause. (3) Stretch–step (to go by), (4) stretch-change up- explode as if to go by, then quick stop.

(Key Point: Lift control foot as if pedaling on a bike. This will allow you to control your foot more easily throughout each frame of a step.)

Foot Control Drills

"3-2-1"drills

With the control foot, simulate each frame of movement as if exploding past the defender: First with three steps, then two and finally one.

(Key point: Start slow then speed up to frenetic pace.)

Dribble Control Drills

"3-2-1" drill

Quarter-step or less: then 3, then 2, and then a single cross.

Hover Dribble

Control foot to range of motion, back to push foot, then to control foot for a long or short step- based on the reaction (movement) of the defender. Repeat for other foot.

(Key point: Maintain change-points. Threaten to go by. Slur the control foot in the air long enough to force reaction from the defender. Continue past with a long step or change directions with a quarter- step or less.)

Hover Changes

Hover, followed by a crossover or between the legs dribble. This helps to maintain continuous hover and range-of-motion action. This is a key default setting for competent ball-handlers.

(Key point: Vary heights of hovers.)

5 phases of "Side–Saddle"
(1) (Chin: Shoulder-to-Shoulder)

From a right hand dribble, move chin clockwise to simulate the start of a spin as your control foot snatches forward.

(Key point: Maintain continuous push foot to control foot in hover mode.)

(2) Slow Spin

Slow controlled forward spin. This allows you to advance with maximum protection, watch the defender and make easy changes according to the position of the defender.

(3) Quick spin

A quick 180° pivot with the feet and body. This allows you to seal the defender with inside shoulder, followed by the quick slam of the outside shoulder.

(Key point: Make sure your chin follows the shoulder over for quicker vision reorientation with the action.)

(4) Half Circle & Back

Half spin and back into original "**side-saddle**" position.

(Key point: Maintain body contact with the defender throughout the spin.)

(5) False Leg

A threatening step forward with body and arm range-of-motion, followed by a stop with the inside or outside foot, sway back. The False leg is effective for mid-range pull-ups.

(Key point: Maintain range- of-motion as long as possible.)

7

PASSING THE TEST

**Intellectually, to be an effective passer, you must
first concern yourself with the 5 W's of passing:
Who, What, When, Where, Why**

What does it take to be an effective passer? Obviously it takes a fundamental understanding of passing, both technical and intellectual. Fundamentally, there are a variety of passes to use to execute ball transport. The two-hand chest or the shovel passes are two examples. The game situation will typically determine the type of pass necessary to complete the transaction successfully. Passing truly is a transaction between two people on the same team with the safeguard of the basketball in the balance.

I believe there is a pass for every game situation that will allow you to employ the **90-10 rule**. If the type of pass does not allow for you to pull the ball back or stop it during the last 10 percent of the delivery, DON'T USE IT! Using that 10 percent space to make sure the pass can be completed effectively will dramatically decrease errant passes and limit turnovers.

The 90-10 rule is different from a ball fake. The 90-10 is more of a mental pause before following through with the pass. Whereas a ball fake is used to deceive the defender, to keep him off balance or at bay. Ball fakes made in the direction of the defender are more effective than ball fakes made side-to-side. Forward fakes force the defender to respond to threat of the ball and lead to open passing lanes. If the defender is up high: up fake, then drop down (change levels) and deliver the ball low. The converse is also true. If the defender drops down low, then fake low and pass high- near the ears area of the defender. Remember: No floaters!

Remember to maintain a **blank screen** as you operate. This means your head and eyes up at rim level. This will broaden your **scope of vision** (the ability to see everything from floor to rim) and allow you to make reads and anticipate plays more quickly. This will also make the defense's ability to read your intentions more difficult. Navigate wisely. Your eyes can be the "window" to your intentions. I am sure you have heard at some point: "DO NOT TELEGRAPH PASSES!"

Let us look closer at the **5 W's:** (1) to **whom** you are passing? (2) **What** type of pass is necessary to complete the transaction successfully? (3) **When** should you pass to her? (4) **Where** should you pass your teammate the ball? (5) **Why** should you pass?

Who you are passing to is a part of **KYP** (Knowing Your Personnel). This and the context of the play should determine **what** kind of pass to deliver. **Extra-passes (EP's)** in search of the best shoot opportunity are great for team success. However, **Over-passes (OP's)** can forfeit a team's best scoring opportunity or any opportunity to score at all. Be sure that passing is the best option for the team in the moment.

When should you pass the ball? Every player should aspire to be a timely passer. It is part of being a good teammate and is one of the keys to effective team offensive. *In a half court set*, you should typically pass to a teammate as she becomes open from the defender. The timing is critical. I often see players hold on to the ball too long, allowing the defender the time to recover, either negating the offensive advantage or, worse, allowing for a steal. *In transition,* the timing of the pass depends on whom you are passing to and their location on the floor. If he can handle the ball in the open-court (particularly a point guard), pass him the ball early so he can spearhead the fast break. If you find a person with lesser ball-handling ability filling the lane, wait to pass him the ball in an area where he can effectively negotiate the space to the basket.

When being pressed, pass to an open teammate before the defense gets to you. DO NOT WAIT TO BE TRAPPED! In fact a ball fake toward a pouncing defender will cause her to pause, giving you a window to make a read and play. If you do find yourself trapped, DO NOT PANIC! Pivot, change levels, or **ball-sweep** (lane to lane) until a passing opportunity presents itself. Trapping defenders are often impatient and prone to fouling. Above all, focus on the security of the basketball. Even if you have to absorb a five second closely guarded violation, it would be better than throwing the ball away and possibly assisting in an easy basket for the opposition. A violation at least allows your team to set up its defense.

Where should you pass the ball to your teammate? Technically, pass the ball to an area that is easy for your teammate to receive and execute after the catch. This is typically the chest or number's area. In terms of Direction, pass the ball to an area that is easy for your teammate to get to yet hard for the defender to get to without a gamble. Too often, passers fail to consider the position of the defense. A target from your teammate should be a start-point for delivery, but be careful: The **90-10 rule** must always be in force. (Note: Before you pass the ball consider whether your teammate will have an opportunity to do something positive after the catch. This will prevent you from passing him into trouble.)

So the question comes back to: should you be passing in the first place or, ***why*** pass? DO NOT PASS JUST TO BE PASSING! Again, EP's to gain the best shot for the team is a productive philosophy. However, OP's can actually forfeit the best opportunity. Be sure that the pass fits within a particular strategy that will lead to the best opportunity for the team that trip. A pass should be a communication between individuals on the same team for strategic gain. It is important to communicate clearly and with purpose. Every time you make a pass, you are risking possession of the team jewel. Be wise.

8

Obviously open

According to the math, and if all things were equal, each player on a five-person team would have the ball twenty percent of the time. Okay, so what happens during the other eighty percent of the time?

Moving effectively without the ball is a highly underemphasized aspect of offensive play - particularly in the American basketball model. I respect coaches who demand attention to strategic movement without the ball from players, and players who put it to good use. Too many players operate as if they are only on offense when they have the basketball. Tragically many players stand around (spotting up?) or watching and waiting for their turn to get the ball.

Is it the mission of the other players to get you the ball? And if it is...are you maximizing each opportunity? I find that players are generally interested in scoring themselves. Some are selfish, but most are just confident in their own ability to score and are not maliciously dominating the ball. I am certain that everyone deep down wants to be the player with the big stats...as long as the team is winning. Sounds great, but first you will have to coax your teammates into passing you the ball. Point guards are not off the hook either. It is true, you usually have the ball every trip; but typically, your first job is to initiate offense. Once you pass the ball, you also become pass-dependent. An effective and team-healthy way to increase touches is to stay **obviously open**. If you are constantly open to make a play and your teammates consistently miss you with passes, then that should be a matter for the coach to resolve.

Are you satisfied with the typical number of passes you receive in games? Most players could use a few more quality touches. A **quality touch** is not just receiving the ball. It is receiving the ball with an opportunity and the time to make productive plays without forcing the action. Forcing the action caters to the defense and compromises offensive connectivity.

What the offensive player needs most is space (**operating time**) away from the defender. There are two situations by which an offensive player can create this space off the catch, with or without screens. Both require proper **scope of vision** of the defender and sound footwork. Proper scope of vision means constant visual contact with the opponent, including the entire range from his feet to the rim simultaneously. This not only broadens the scope to include teammates, gaps and passing lanes, but it also fuses anticipation and expectation. The sooner visual contact is made - particularly on the defender's feet – the sooner you can gain an understanding of the defender's intentions. This will grant you more time or, more perception of time, to negotiate. In other words, it slows the game down to a more manageable level. This is a the key to processing play effectively and playing under control - particularly in the face of high-speed encounters such as being **closed out** on or otherwise harassed by defenders.

There are some similarities between getting open with or without screens. The timing of movements to the basket and the manipulation of the opponent with the feet and body are the same. As the ball-handler initiates movement to the left or right side of the court and approaches the delivery area, you should begin a straight-line assault (**V-cut**) to the basket. Be sure to time your back-cut or pop-out to the wing to coincide with the ball-handler's ability to deliver the basketball. This reduces the recovery time of your defender and promotes smooth-running offensive team play.

On your assault, if the defender does not defend your movement toward the basket and stays still, then continue to the basket for a backdoor lay-in. Move straight past the defender with your body to seal the backdoor area; moving away allows him to recover. If the defender defends the basket, then abruptly change directions (v-cut) and flare to the wing or fade to the baseline for a catch. Continue to watch the defender even after the initial read and course of action; you may need to make an adjustment yet.

Making defenders choose a course of action, then doing something different is known as keeping them in **choice position** or being contrary. This is the essence of manipulating any confrontation to your advantage. In the end, manipulation comes down to false intention based on the battle of the feet between you and the defender. Thankfully, defenders are required to take whole steps to shut down routes. Therefore, any fraction of a step you are able to negotiate in one direction creates a space advantage or allows you to be first in the other direction contrary to the defender's movement.

Another method to create space without screens is the use of **L-cuts**. An L-cut starts with a quick V-cut followed by a movement straight up (towards the ball), then over and away from the defender in a strict $90°$ angle to receive the ball. If properly timed, you can create quite a bit of closeout space this way. You can also seal the defender with your body, move where you have to go, then extend over sharply just before the ball arrives. This method creates less space from the defender, but is a more surefire way to get open in a crunch.

Getting open with screens is like having a personal assistant to help you score. Any time a screen comes your way, value it as a golden opportunity to be productive. Proper use of screens will certainly increase your offensive opportunities. Using screens starts in the same manner as above - with a timely V-cut to force the defender back toward the basket. The screener and receiver (you) assault the block area as the dribbler chooses a particular side and starts to move into a delivery area. As the screener nears, stop your assault abruptly and move back toward the screener as closely as possible. This will force the defender to choose a defensive tactic or direction. Rub shoulders with the screener - if possible - and proceed exactly opposite of the defender at the point of the screen.

Moving opposite the defender will produce effective screen options: **curls** to the basket, **flares** to the wing, and **fades** to the baseline - or any combination of the three. This is why it is hugely important to watch the defender throughout. It makes situational adjustments more valid relative to the defender or defense, and keeps you in constant control of the game speed. Constant vision on the defender sounds easy, but it is even easier not to do. Force yourself to keep an eye on your man for the entire sequence.

On backdoor cuts:

Whether your advantage is to continue to the basket on a **slip** or return to the basket on a back-cut, try to stop around the box area for the catch. This allows you access to the backboard, maximizes the spacing between you and the next help defender, and preserves your ability to make a pass to your teammate – if necessary.

On flaring or fading to the perimeter:

Another approach is to force the defender back toward the basket with adamant threats to go backdoor. With a solid V-cut, this will give you an opportunity to catch the ball on the perimeter. If the defender returns too quickly out to deny the pass, then proceed once again backdoor for the lay-up.

All this should be done on a straight-line from block to wing and vice versa. Leaving the path to get open caters to the defense. It adds more steps and frames to your movements and therefore wastes time. Remember: It is not the quantity of touches you receive that matters, as much as it is the quality of touches you receive during play.

9

Lane Play

The Law of Leadership in basketball is the right of the offensive player to dictate or act first relative to the defender. The offensive player knows his intentions and the defender does not. Therefore the defender must respect any of his threats to go by or shoot over him. This means, as the offensive player, you have the power to control the defender by prompting him into a certain action, then responding contrary to whatever he does. This is the key to staying ahead of the opponent or being "first."

Lane Play is simply the art of operating effectively - **off-the-catch** or **off-the-dribble.** Developing it will make you a master manipulator and productive within any system of play. Lane play starts with getting yourself *obviously open* at a spot where you are a threat to score – if possible. Only then are you in true triple-threat position. Catching beyond from where you can shoot puts you in double-threat position at best. *Obviously open* should always include constant vision on the defender to promote early awareness of his intentions. Optimally, you should already be set and have an idea of how to prompt the defender into an action by the time you receive the ball. This keeps you ahead of the defender or **first,** and gives you an opportunity to be contrary or manipulative.

> *The anatomy of an offensive move*: **The offensive player is first or A. The defender gets to respond as B. Now, the offensive player gets to "C" what to do and be contrary. Learn to slow down and allow the defender to be B.**

To stay **first** focus on preparing your feet and body for action before you receive the ball. That includes being on balance – ready to spring up, to shoot or explode past. Getting prepared before the catch is known as **catching at zero** or **sticking the landing**. This means absolutely no time to get set after receiving the ball whatsoever. This is critical because there is typically only about a half second or less of **closeout space** between you and the approaching defender. Getting set quickly maximizes this space and gives you an opportunity to be productive within the same context of your teammates. In the "context of your teammates" refers to being productive in the flow of or within the continuity of a particular offensive set without just going one-on-one.

After the catch, an upward ball fake will demand a reaction from the defender closing-out. The movement simulates all phases of triple-threat-shooting, passing and driving in the early frames. This will force the defender to stop, pause or lunge. (Note: The key is to threaten the defender in the earliest possible frames of the exchange. The sooner you threaten, the sooner you establish control.)

If the defender stops and is beyond your **meter-box** (safe-zone for a non-rushed shot attempt), take the shot and expect to make it. If you see the defender start to lunge forward, immediately make provisions to get past him to the next spot on the path. There is no reason to try and speed past. Since a lunging defender is traveling opposite of your movement, he is vulnerable to you moving past him. Getting past is actually a matter of getting your body (specifically, your shoulder) on the defender and maintaining leverage against him. This **straight-cut** will get you where you need to be quickly and under control.

There are three operational lanes relative to the defender (Diagram 6A). *Lane 1* is your strong-hand side alley. *Lane 2* is the cage area for shooting - when in range and passing. *Lane 3* is the weak-side alley past the defender.

It is not always possible to catch at zero. There are times when you will be forced to catch the ball at an angle away from the basket and defender. When this is the case a **power square-up** will keep you in a superior position based on the defender. A power square-up is a sweeping of the arms and ball along with a pivot to face up and threaten the defender. On the right side, start the ball in the left lane, so the sweep will be toward the basket. Be sure to include the left lane (lane 1) to go by the defender. The middle lane (lane 2) is to shoot or pass. Finally, as you continue to sweep to the right lane (lane 3), do not forget to allow the defender to act (or to be **B**) before you actually proceed. It is important to threaten the lane you receive the ball in first - if only for one frame of movement.

Range-of-Motion (**ROM**) is the process of changing levels toward the defender, while also preparing your feet for forward movement. ROM satisfies the early frames of movement, to go by or to at least breech into his defensive space. This forces the defender to react or allow you to continue past in the direction of the threat — either right or left. If the defender chooses to guard a lane, you should be able to slip past him (blade first) in the other lane. At the very least, this should give you enough control to mislead, change directions, and/or pull up for a shot anywhere along the path to the basket.

In fact, the in-between or mid-range shot is a potent weapon: First, it is an easy shot to make. And second, it forces defensive help, which can lead to even easier shot for the team. Moreover, if the catch is done correctly - at zero - then your eyes and mind (which serve as your personal radar system) will have locked on to your off-the-catch location in terms of distance from the rim. The makes the mid-range shot seem like a chippie in the next moment. It is similar to the relative ease of the second free throw after a successful first free throw.

Bottom line: If you have a good shot, take it. If you can proceed further to put more pressure on the defense and possibly get a better shot for the team, then by all means proceed. Always exploit your greatest offensive advantage in the moment until it is necessary to do otherwise.

The team goal, on each offensive trip beyond getting a lay-up, should be to get the next best shot for the team. An open look from twenty feet by a capable shooter is usually a good shot - unless someone has a better opportunity. It is all about reads and making the correct choices. A ten-foot shot from a player who struggles from ten feet is not a better opportunity for the team. Deep penetration may get a person closer to the basket, but does it create a better opportunity for the team? Driving, drawing help, and dishing can be great for a team and for overall moral. However, passing up an easy shot or lay-up just to include teammates is counter-productive. The team goal must be finding the best shooting opportunity for the team each trip down the floor.

In summary: V-cut or L-cut to create operating space. Get your feet and body around in position to shoot or drive as soon as possible - ideally before the catch. If not, the power square up applies. Always know where the defender is. Up-fake to force the defender into a response. Shoot if the defender is outside your meter-box and you are in true triple threat position. If he bites on the up-fake and lunges forward to contest the shot, then "body" past into the next read under control, in pursuit of the middle spot. If the defense cannot contest the middle spot, then take the shot and knock it down. If the next defender approaches to contest, then you should be able to make a pass to a teammate for an easy look.

Staying in your lane puts maximum pressure on the defense because it gets you where you need to go quickly, under control and better able to execute options. Put lane play to use. It is your opportunity to be productive every touch you get.

10

Line drive

On a drive to the basket, seek to neutralize the opponent with dominant bodywork as quickly as possible to allow the proper read of the situation. Either pull-up at the middle spot (spot 2), or continue towards the knee-up spot (spot 3), the take-off spot (spot 4) or the reverse spot (spot 5). Just make sure you read before you proceed

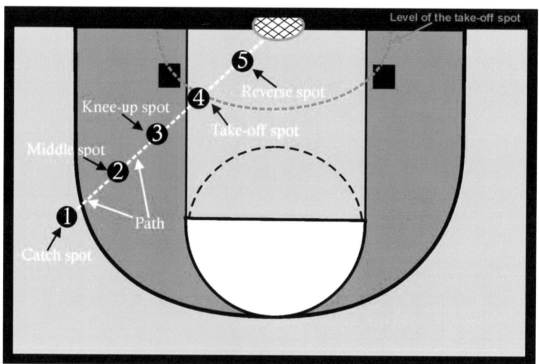

Diagram 10A

There are 5 spots along the path to the basket: (1) **the catch spot**, (2) **the middle spot**, (3) **the knee-up spot**, (4) **the lay-up spot,** and (5) **the reverse spot** (See Diagram 10A). Acquaint yourself with these operational spots. Travel along the path at a speed that allows you to weigh your options at every "stop" along the path. Never volunteer to leave the path. Staying on the **road** and using your body will help you maintain control over your man and force the help to come over in a drastic way. This will make it easy for you to find an open teammate.

I bet, like most players, you probably feel that you are beyond the need for lay-up mechanics. The truth is you probably should be, but it may not be the case. Even if you are a polished finisher this section will at least remind you of something you already know or do. Solid lay-up mechanics are an extremely important yet undervalued aspect of basketball. Poor mechanics leads to botched offensive opportunities and extra opportunities for the defense. There should be more consideration. Across all levels of play, the team that makes the most lay-ups usually wins - especially in youth basketball.

Part of how you make the most lay-ups is by finishing all the ones presented throughout the course of the game - both contested and non-contested. At a bare-minimum, a non-contested lay-in requires the right read of the defense, a reasonable take-off spot, and proper use of the backboard. We will discuss backboard spots next chapter in "Backboard Mastery."

Because of the defensive pressure, a contested lay-up requires more. After gauging the intentions and proximity of the defender, the next movement should be slightly towards the defender yet straight to the basket. Moving slightly toward the defender allows you to dominate the **inner space** and control the defender with body leverage. When going to the basket with a defender next to you or in the near vicinity always think about "**body first**." In fact, you should body-hunt with your shoulder as soon as possible. The fundamental of moving your inside hand over (**hand-to-ball**) bulges the shoulder blade toward the defender and prepares you for contact, if necessary. If a collision is imminent, move toward defender and flex immediately on contact. Once contact has been made, continuing to lean towards the defender helps you maintain leverage and control. Make sure you stabilize (flex again) on the ground before going up for the shot. If there is excessive contact, the foul will generally go against the defender. Many times – despite the foul - you will still be stable enough to finish the play.

There are times when you get to the take-off spot and may not need to use your body to secure the lay-up. Try not to compromise your take-off spot just for the sake of body hunting. However it is healthy to have a body hunter's mentality. Finally, be ready to execute whatever necessary line drive maneuver (mentioned below) on your path to the basket.

Bump & Go (Flex and Finish)

The quicker you can get your body against the defender on final approach the better chance you have of limiting the defender's capacity to make a positive play. If contact is made near the box area, you should bump and flex toward the defender to absorb the impact; then continue leaning against the defender as you move toward the basket for the finish.

Ball-Tuck

On final approach, if the defender approaches aggressively toward your direct line to the basket, a ball-tuck maneuver will change your speed and create space relative to the defender. On the first of the final two steps to the basket move the ball up through the shooting zone, past the head and down toward the back of the neck. At this point you should be able to gauge the defender's action and determine your advantage in time for the next step.

The entire ball-tuck movement may not be necessary, however. You may find advantage during any point of the maneuver: possibly for a **runner** or to continue past toward the basket.

Ball Tuck to Knee-up

In "Lane Play" we talked about the knee-up spot in terms of a location – the area along the path to the basket between the middle spot and take-off spot. Now let us talk about knee-ups in terms of strategy of use and mechanics. Knowing when to use the knee-up spot versus the take-off spot adds another dimension to successful drive negotiation.

Knee-ups ill-time the defenders jump, giving the offensive player first use of the airspace to the basket. On final approach, plant the take-off foot and raise the opposite knee up while simultaneously moving hands up through the shooting zone above the head. This action will create separation from the defender, lift and suspend the player, allowing for easy backboard use, "runner" capability, and pass options.

In a two-on-one final approach scenario, this maneuver puts the defender in a quandary or "choice position." This means having to choose whether to leap to contest the shot or stay down and protect the passing lane from the ball-handler she initially thought she was guarding. An out-of-control ballplayer is barely safer than any other out-of-control vehicle, particular when it comes to damage. Line Drive takes the hurry and rush out of drives to the basket, keeping you under control and better able to make positive plays.

Lane Change

On final approach with the defender close and threatening to take your direct line to the basket away, shift the ball to the other side of your body and lean the former ball-side shoulder against the defender, and continue to the basket. The technically-clean version would be to keep your shoulders straight and maintain a forward course on the line to the basket. Shift the ball from lane to lane as the defender moves off the line, then lean with the shoulder to keep him sealed.

Ode to an offensive weapon

If you've got a shot- make it.

If you've got a drive- take it.

If you've got a pass- relay it

11

BACKBOARD MASTERY

Diagram 11A

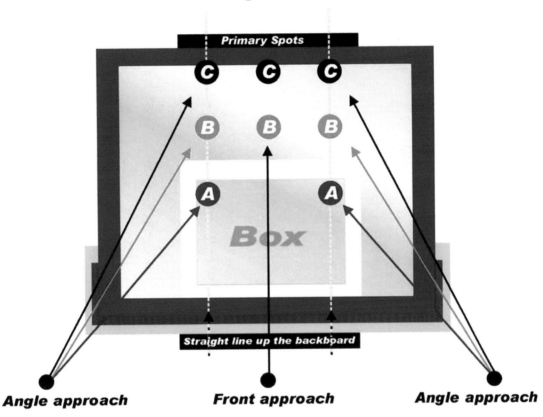

Using the backboard to make shots is not the offensive staple it once was. Sure, as modern-day backboard shooters, "The Big Fundamental" comes to mind. But the prevalence of backboard masters are from an era gone by. That is unfortunate, given the additional offensive opportunities of effective backboard use. Using the glass effectively expands your repertoire of shots and allows you to make shots moving at different angles and speeds. It also allows you to shoot higher and quicker without compromising accuracy and touch, which is essential to finishing over defenders on final approach. Using the glass will make you a resourceful scorer in and around the paint and provide more options on mid range shots. Learning to use the backboard is no different than learning to use any other instrument: it requires practice and precision. This chapter breaks down the keys for effective backboard use regardless of your distance from the basket.

There are 3 **primary spots** on each side of the basket and two more above it, to use to successfully bank the ball into the basket. See: Diagram 10 A. On angled drives or approaches *Spot A* (located just inside the top corner of the box), *Spot B* (on the same line six inches above the box), and *Spot C* (on the line near the top of backboard) are primary targets. When driving straight on, aim six inches above the box to the top of the board (**Spot B** and **C**). Determining which spot to use should be based on your location and the position and pressure of the defender(s). Three **secondary spots** (Diagram 11B) can be effective with reverse spins, but are more difficult to execute.

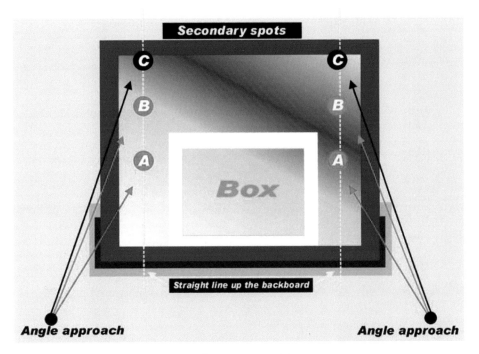

Diagram 11B

Understand that the action off the glass is not a throw, but rather a **kiss** or soft spin against the backboard. The higher the spot, the softer the kiss should be. Therefore, spot A would allow for the fastest paced shot. The eyes must be trained to identify and focus on the spots and the body must follow through to hit them. There is no substitute for watching the ball go through the hoop and knowing which spot and ball speed will make it happen. Backboard mastery is a valuable tool for your "tool box".

12

"D" or Die?

Tell me the last time you heard of or saw a player stick out his chest and say, "I got D", as a way to represent himself?

It seems fewer people truly understand the science of defense. How many players today are actually interested in playing it? Maybe it is as simple as defense or **"D"** being so physically and mentally demanding. Maybe no one is willing to do the dirty work for a task with seemingly such little star power. How many ads do you see top defenders in? Who wears their Jerseys? I hear about "mad hops", "wet" jumpers, crazy crossovers and even show stoppers - which by the way, has nothing to do with actually stopping anybody defensively - it is typically reserved for the guy who had the nastiest dunk or maybe the greatest assortment of off-the-dribble trickery.

Are you defensive-minded? Do you take pride in stopping your man? Are you contributing to your team defensively? It is a basic reality: either your opponent is dictating the interplay between the two of you, or you are. No one said defense is easy and it is not, but there are methods to effective play.

Part of that formula for defense is intelligence on offense: NEVER WASTE OFFENSIVE POSSESSIONS. Make your opponent work. Making your opponent responsible (spend energy) on defense gives them less actual time for offense. That is a defensive consideration, even though it is offense. How you play offense will ultimately impact the way the other team plays offense or gets to play offense. Whatever the case, offense should be a part of your defensive strategy. Moreover, offense should begin with how you play defense. Are you with me?

Putting the ball in the basket may be the most glamorous part of the game, but defense has and will always be the key to victory. On most teams the best defensive player usually gets ample playing time. The best defensive teams often get rewarded with victories. Is it a coincidence that Bill Russell - arguably the best defensive player in basketball history - also has the most championship rings? Jordan and Pippen were also great defenders. How many rings do they have between them? Still, the list of defensive stalwarts is short. Everybody wants to win the championship, but just like most who want to go to heaven, few want to walk the narrow road of the righteous and even fewer willing to endure the sacrifices required to become a top defender.

I respect players and coaches who focus their attention on both ends of the court- especially defensive rebounding (See: "Bound Together," Chapter 13). Without the rebound you are still on D. How many coaches truly stress either or make their players responsible for both? Too often, it is all about the show offensively: *"Watch me work, hear the roar, defense is for those who can't score."* Even if not the pre-game plan, too often it ends up being the case.

Today, offensive abilities are off the chart. Unfortunately, defensive prowess has not kept pace. Somehow there has been a devaluation of defensive accountability at all levels of the game. If you find yourself in an environment that places emphasis on defensive play, consider yourself fortunate. In defense of the "defensively challenged", many players manage to figure out offense - if only by themselves: a ball, a basket, *voila!* This chapter is designed to make you a better defensive player and a more valuable defensive component for your team. Defense is largely a mental endeavor, but there is no escaping the physical elements. To play man-on-man defense, you must first be aware of the proper stance, and use of the feet and body. Stance gives you the absolute speed we talked about in Chapter 3. Establishing an **anchor foot** and a **snatch foot** in conjunction with range-of–motion allows you to prepare to move in a certain direction in the early frames without committing your feet to movement and thereby compromising your position. The anchor foot is similar to the push foot on offense. The snatch foot is similar to the control foot (See Chapter 5). Always be willing to exhaust your range-of–motion before committing to a movement. This will make you less inclined to overreact to fakes or stunts and will give you the defensive security to eventually *"hawk your man"*: fight to take away his "leadership" and force your will. We will touch on *Hawking* below. The education on defense starts with going to **S.C.H.O.O.L.**

S = Size

Size him up. What are his tendencies? Does he prefer to operate going right or left? What is his dominant hand? What type of shooter, with what kind of range? Which direction is he more comfortable getting his shot off? Is he a good ball handler? What about his physical attributes? Does he have foot speed/quickness? These are the type of questions to ask when evaluating your opponent and devising a strategy (size-up) to defend him. If you have a scouting-report at your disposal, use that in addition to an on-the-spot appraisal to forge a strategy. Anything you can come up with can and should be used against them. However, make sure your strategy is in alignment with the overall team defensive strategy. For example, if you determine that your man prefers to go right and the specific team strategy is to force him right, then force him right applying the principles we will discuss next.

C = CONTROL

At some point you are going to have to move your feet...quickly. Getting your feet (legs) up to speed is no easy proposition. Defensive slides must be done to the point of tremendous burn and fatigue to condition your legs for the task. It takes courage and dedication to grind out this type of mobility. Over time your legs will gain the ability to move rapidly, make quick starts and changes on command. Jumping rope - speed jumping in particular - can increase your dexterity, agility and overall Spider-Man like qualities, which will further increase your physical ability to defend.

Slides start with proper stance (Diagram 12A). Start from basic triple threat position: wide stance, knees bent, butt out and back straight, arms should be out towards the defender. Make sure you are not flatfooted or back on your heels. You should be up on your push pads in **bounce position**, ready to move. Be certain to maintain a low body level and the distance between your feet. Keeping your feet apart allows you to defend more territory and able to change directions more quickly than otherwise. To slide imagine a vertical line running down the center of your body. To begin your movement, focus on pulling yourself from that center point over in the intended direction. Be sure to snatch your foot over in the direction you intend to go then push with your anchor foot to continue in that direction.

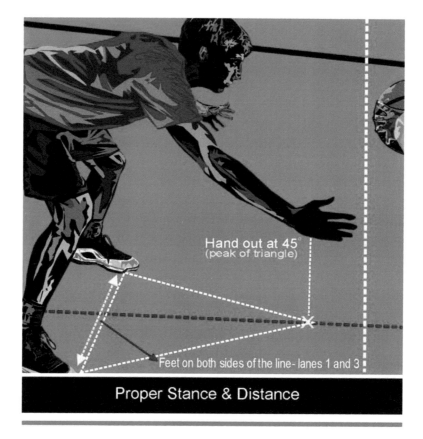

Diagram 12A

Now that your legs can move like pistons, you are ready to do your part to help protect the basket (The Queen)- i.e., to stop the opponent from scoring. This starts by *controlling* your man or stopping him or her from driving past you, right? First, set up in your defensive stance. The standard distance from the offensive player is arms length away or touching distance. If you are as fast as or faster than the offensive player then you can afford to guard at arms length from the body. (Notice his distance from the ball in Diagram 11). If you are not as fast, keep yourself at arms distance from the ball. Whichever the case, NEVER COMPROMISE THAT SPACE! Guarding too closely makes it easier for a smart or speedy player to get past you. Plus you are easier to fake out of position.

66

The goal is to force or **shade** a player to a particular side or lane. To shade, position yourself diagonally (at 45°) in both the driving lane of the side you wish to deny entry and lane 2. Covering lane 2 allows you to contest shots as well. For example, if you want to force your man to the left side, setup in right driving lane with your inside foot positioned in the middle of lane 2 or in the center of his body. Remember you are trying to control him or at the very least, make him less comfortable than being allowed to operate in his preferred direction. Unless you shade or take away a side, you are basically giving a player access to both lanes at once. Defense is tough enough. Take away a side to reduce your defensive coverage area and to give your teammates a better opportunity to hedge (anticipate) how to help.

Do not confuse shading with conceding the other side. You shade to shut down one lane, but compete with sound Range-of-Motion and to take away the other. You can increase your effectiveness to shut down lanes by playing **Common spot defense**.

Common spot defense focuses on fighting to defend the shared spot along the path to the basket. For example, if the offensive player begins to drive right, your goal should be to pivot and snatch to beat the player to a spot on the path that lies behind you to the basket. Never move forward or slide sideways when threatened. Not only will you be moving away from the basket, but you will also compromise good position as well. (See: arms distance rule). In that scenario, you will probably find yourself trying to stop penetration with your body or by reaching in, which will quickly lead to unnecessary fouling. Therefore, it is vitally important to defend the common spot. If you are in good position, you should be able to get there first. If your opponent is a poor shooter, then you might be able to back up a bit further and entice a shot or to delay or discourage a drive. This is not about granting your opponent anything. If a player commits to a shot, do everything in your power to contest without fouling. Complete your effort with a solid box out and possible pursuit of a rebound.

Arms distance and common spot defense make it easier to control your man. It keeps you away at a distance that helps you contain penetration, yet close enough to challenge the dribble space and contest shots.

H = Hawk and Harass

There is no reason to be passive on defense. You are not providing a luxury tour. Your mission is to keep your opponent uncomfortable and under control. Great footwork and positioning keeps you in front of your man, but hawking and harassing play is the next level of discombobulating activity. Body or lunge fakes, sometimes even vocal distractions can be effective ploys to keep your opponent off balance. **Strategic touching** can also help limit your man's overall effectiveness. Sometimes a strategic touch is necessary to halt progress and allow you to maintain arms length. This is not to advocate continuous holding or making hand-use the rule, but rather an occasional touch to re-register your position - with your feet. Hawking the ball with your hands makes passing and shooting more difficult. In fact, a hand above the ball will actually deter shots and provide you an angle to strip the ball away.

Perhaps the most important aspect of hawking is the relentless effort to deny him a pass in the first place. Denials requires no more energy or even less energy than it takes to allow your man to get the ball and then have to guard him - especially if he is a crafty scorer or tough to stay in front of. Deny your man the ball every chance you get and take note of his response. Many times not getting touches will increase his anxiety, limit other contributions, and induce poor decision-making. How many times have you seen a player get limited - if any - touches for a time period, then take a bad shot or make an ill-advised play the next time he touches the ball? Denials are tough work, but a relatively small price to pay to be in the mind of your opponent. It pains me to see three or four players buy into that type of play, while others allow their man to receive passes. It renders any defense less effective, and wastes team energy. It will irritate any knowledgeable coach and most likely cost you playing time. If you are too tired to play defense the right way, there is usually free room and board (i.e. the bench and some water) on the sideline. Hopefully you will get a nice towel too.

It is true that offense has its advantages in basketball, but that does not mean you have to be the victim on defense. You should always try to be the aggressor while staying mindful of your disadvantages and limitations. Respect the fact that someone else may be quicker, faster or whatever. Adjust to your advantage, whatever that may be. The truth is many teams and offensive players give away their advantages time and again with unnecessary dribbling, poor footwork, bodywork and lack of understanding about strategic spacing on the floor. So much of defense is about the willingness to play it and the will power to maintain it.

O = Obey Defensive Principles

How consumed are players with defensive principles? Most players often hear directives such as stay at arms length or at touching distance. Guarding with your belly is a recipe for fouling or a breech to the basket. Are you sensitive to guarding the common spot or do ball fakes and jabs move you side-to-side or lunging forward? Never **double guard** with your feet and destroy your positioning to the basket. Instead, back up on threats to maintain this proper spacing.

What about the hand above the ball rule? This keeps you in position to deter and contest shots. What about jumping to the ball side after your man passes it? Do you **bump and greet** your man instead of following behind him towards the basketball? Do you break your feet down on closeouts or do you leap out and make quick retreats not possible? What about something as simple as falling down to take charges? Defensive principles in use will only add to your effectiveness as a defender. Learn and apply as many as possible. Remember to talk on defense. Not trash-talk, but rather communicate with your teammates as part of the collective mission to get stops.

O = Operate Strategy

Organize, operate and stay focused on individual and team strategy for defense. Adjustments should be made whenever necessary. The goal is to be more solid than a risk taker on D. There will be opportunities to make plays (steals). Choose your battles wisely. Ask yourself if the risk is worth the consequence. Never rest on defense. If you find yourself on the floor, find it inside yourself to defend whether on ball or in "help." To me, a player unwilling to play D is selfish. Loves to shoot, loves to score... but doesn't mind his man scoring and letting his team down - Please! He is no winner.

L = Lock your man up

If you work to apply all the principles we have discussed in this section, you will no doubt enjoy greater success on defense. These principles will give you an opportunity to contain your man and contribute big-time to any team's defensive scheme. It truly is about your intensity, your intelligence and your resolve to get it done. Stellar D will definitely get the attention of the coaches. It may not always get you the publicity you deserve or privately desire, but it will certainly get you more of what all players truly covet: playing time. Trust me.

13

Lane Patrol

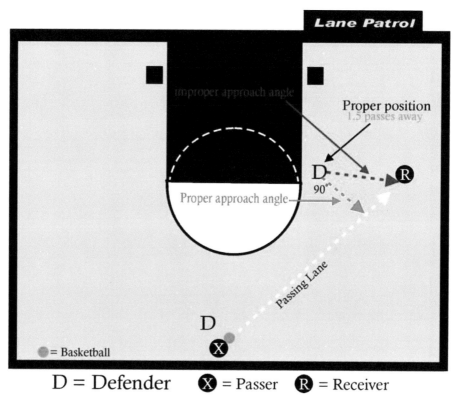

Diagram 13A

Simply and succinctly, **Lane Patrol** is the art of playing the passing lane on defense. Patrol starts from help position, based on your distance from the ball and the **passing lane** - the straight line between the passer and potential receiver. As a help-defender, you should be positioned in the center of a 90° vortex created by one arm pointing at the center of your man and the other pointing at the center of the ball and its handler. This makes seeing your man and the ball at the same time easier, and positions you ahead of your man relative both to the ball and basket. The further away the ball, the further you should move towards the basket into help position.

One pass away is strict denial. This is arguably the most disruptive element of defense. Two or more passes away is help position: as close to the basket as possible to help protect, yet close enough to your man to be able to recover and defend. There is no reason for anyone to hug her man ever. The proper help position is towards the ball, based on the number of passes away it is from your man. This is **Rule 1.** Obeying this rule will give you the confidence and security to position yourself to "help" properly and to recover efficiently.

Proper positioning is like getting a head start to where you need to be. It helps take the guesswork out of what course of action to make a play. More importantly, your reads, assessments, and actions will sharpen and you will make better decisions in the heat of the action. Still patrol abuses run rampant in today's basketball society. I see it all the time: a player who almost comes up with the ball on a steal attempt and shouts, "My bad" after the opposition capitalizes off the miscue. You can make the play with **(Rule 2)** - the proper angle approach. Moving perpendicular toward the passing lane is more efficient than racing the ball the longer distance of 45° to the man (Diagram 13 A). Poor reads and poor technique on patrol lead to power plays for the opposition and gray hairs for the coaching staff.

Rule 3: Extend the arm closest to the passer on denials and deflection attempts. This puts your arm substantially closer to the ball than the receiver; and as a plus, if the ball does happen to slip past your hand to the receiver you are still in legitimate position to defend. This technique all but eliminates **flybys** (or, running past the receiver into no-man's land on failed steal attempts). Flybys typically involve an improper approach angle to the passing lane.

This is your duty as a patrol officer. Deny like crazy and make the plays (steals) that come your way. Be prudent in your decision-making concerning risks that can adversely impact your team. **Rule 4**: Always lean towards containment in lieu of trying to steal the ball. Solid citizenry on patrol is all a coach is really looking for. A steal can be a big momentum play. Just make sure you are stealing the ball and not the life out of the defense. Most sheriffs (coaches) will take you off duty for offenses like that.

14

Protect the Queen

Each player must guard (on-ball) to the max, and help (off-ball) to the max in defense of the Queen. Allowing entry into her chamber without every effort to secure it is unforgivable and punishable by benching.

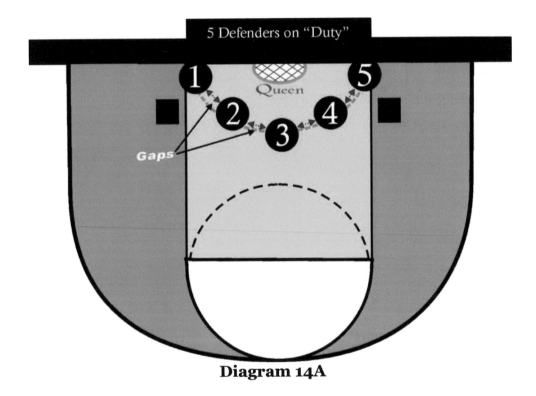

Diagram 14A

Protect the Queen is a team mentality of working together defensively to disallow any easy or uncontested attempt fired upon her majesty, the Queen. The Queen is the basket. When you are on defense you are on duty. Defense of her requires communication, solid technique, proper motivation, discipline, tenacity and a whatever-it–is-to-do mentality to get stops. Of course, any flagrant activity lies outside the rules of engagement. "D or

Die" (Chapter 12) outlines the basics of on-ball defense. This section centers on individual defensive responsibilities inside the team scope.

In the diagram above you see all five players in an arc (on duty) protecting the "Queen." As they step forward the space between them widens and creates lanes or gaps. Stopping penetration into these lanes is essential to a lockdown defensive unit. Gap management is about closing these gaps as opposing players try to breech security and get to basket - with or without the ball. The player with the ball has obvious power but players without the basketball are also dangerous as they seek entry into the chamber with backdoor cuts, slips and curls. Stopping these assaults is no easy proposition. All five players must be responsible for the ball at all times and filling gaps when necessary. You are either on the ball, denying your man the chance to receive it, or in help position to protect the basket against easy lay-ups. Quality coaches hold players accountable for breakdowns in all three categories.

Help Tips: In a zone set, each player is responsible to defend the ball, an area and the basket. In a man-to-man situation, it is ball, man and basket.

Never allow your man in between you and the ball. In fact, try not to let your man run free. **Bumping and Greeting (B&G)** cutters is essential to gap management. **B&G** is not about actually hitting a player per se, but rather about getting in his path to disrupt his primary route. **B&G** will stop that player's surge and allow you to reset (moving toward the ball) and maintain optimal position. Identifying and bumping cutters is critically important in zone sets.

Gap Management

As the ball-handler approaches your lane, the on-ball defender must continue to defend his man in anticipation of help. Too many times the on-ball defender relaxes and over relies on the help defense. The helper must move over - not up - to close the gap and thwart penetration of the dribbler. **Helping-up** moves the defender away from the basket and makes him vulnerable to backdoor cuts by his man. **Helping-over** allows the defender to shut down the lane, yet positioned still to recover to his assigned man. It may be helpful to think about it mathematically. You should help-over to create a 90° angle with the on-ball-defender as the dribbler drives him back towards the basket. Be certain to close the gap with your feet and body and prepare to take a charge if necessary. Reaching in to make a play or lying back to block shots near the basket leads to unnecessary breeches, fouls and ultimately free throws for the opposition.

The defensive unit is only as solid as its weakest link. Good teams will inevitably exploit any such shortcoming. Sometimes it may take extra effort on top of effort to meet the defensive objective. So be it. The protection of the *Queen* is at stake.

15

"Bound" Together

Is the rebound the most vital part of a defensive stop?
Without it, you are still on "D".

It is beautiful to watch the synchronized efforts of a defensive unit determined to protect the Queen down to the nth degree. Whatever the circumstance on D, protection is not complete until the ball has been apprehended (rebounded). Each player must be responsible for boxing out his man or someone in the area every time the ball goes up. Bottom line: No second chance attempts (shots) on the Queen. Poor rebounding teams are rarely championship-caliber teams. Allowing offensive rebounds grants extra opportunities and often leads to easy second-chance shots. Securing the rebound rewards the team for its defensive effort and puts them in position for offensive gain. Many times a team's most dangerous offensive weapon is the opportunistic fast break, which does not exist without solid rebounding. "Bounding together" is about accountability from each player every time a shot goes up.

The strategy for rebounding starts with **P&P: Probability and Proximity**. Probability is the summation of facts to determine the likely destination of the ball following a missed shot. Proximity is a strategy for getting as close as you can, as soon as you can, to that location. There is a lot to process when the ball goes up and little time to act. It is not always possible to get there, but certainly make sure your man does not either. It is a work of art to watch all five players seal off and create an inner sanctum for the ball to drop. If everyone boxes out, the chance of your team getting the ball is high, particularly on defense. Pivot, shift, lean, or do whatever to seal your man off and give yourself a chance to retrieve the ball. Obviously you cannot grab or shove, but...

The first tenet for probability is to identify the location of the shooter. Long shots often produce long rebounds and many times they ricochet opposite the shooter. Now factor in the rate of the shooter. Is he stationary or is it a runner? What are the tendencies of the shooter? How was the previous shot attempt missed? What is the shot pressure (defensive and emotional)? Is it a contested or open look? What is the game context? Is it a crucial play? Learn to process these and any other factors that may help determine a flight pattern and pending location for a rebound. Next, shift your attention to the release of the ball. Just as a center fielder must focus on the ball as it leaves the bat, it is equally as important to watch the flight of the ball from the fingertips of the shooter. It is the most powerful predictor of rebound location.

Now it is time to **Box** (seal the opposition) and **Go** (retrieve the ball). Too many times players *box* out, but do not *go* get the ball. Ideally, you seal off in order to explode first to the ball. It is important to extend up to the level of the ball as opposed to letting the ball fall down to you. Waiting for the ball to come to you risks deflections in the dead space between your standing level and the rebound level. Going after the ball with one hand allows you to extend further. However, the other hand must come over quickly to secure the ball.

The absolute moment the ball is touched, look to locate an outlet person or *flyer*. Your head should be coming around to look even before you land. The window for advantage closes quickly and early recognition and delivery maximizes any fast break or breakaway opportunities.

Offensive rebounding requires the same principles of the two P's (Probability and Proximity) mentioned earlier. Identify the likely rebound area and fight to get there. Look to seal your man - to the inside for the rights to long rebounds. Assume every shot is a miss. If you do come up with a rebound, please treat each offensive-rebound with the same value as any other possession. Too often, players are less judicious about the quality of the "extra" shot.   Great teams are often built around maximizing extra possessions. That is what makes great rebounders so special. The correlation between championship teams and dominant rebounding is a logical link.

"Bounding together" will help any team increase its bottom line. To be a part of it is not about how high you can jump, but rather how quickly you can process and employ **P & P** and **B & G**.

16

THE VIRTUAL ARTIST

Welcome to the basketball matrix. Here ultimate technique meets artistic expression. As a Virtual Player, you are bound only by perfection and emotion. Otherwise, there is no limit to your growth and actualization. Actualization as a Virtual Player occurs when you have mastered the art of allowing yourself to demonstrate the full gamut of your skill sets in the moment of exchange.

The road to virtual actualization is an arduous journey. It is truly the road less traveled. It takes incredible brainpower and discipline to deal with the rigors of programming and development: Man vs. Brain is the main event in an emotional "super fight." So few stay the path as the stress and strain of change becomes too difficult and the process outweighs the passion and resolve of the individual. It is understandable. A Virtual Player is a rare treasure and like the most precious stone, the product of proper pressure, focus and time. Pressure to improve steadily. Focus on the right materials. And time to make it all happen.

VP's objectives for play are governed by net result and outcomes. Success is based on established default settings for optimal performance and extreme focus. VP's mental make-up is one of emotional control. This control is rooted in the ability to withstand the toll of programming - interjecting commands to forge positive reps and acquire skill. VP's realize they are greater than the brain and can exercise dominion through hyper-focus and a calm assertive mind. This mastery of the brain game will stand as a purposeful model of understanding advancement for whatever else in life.

As a VP you function as a viable component of any system. You understand that it takes the right inputs for the right outputs and are machine-like in your approach. Intellectually you process the action of the game frame-by-frame, as if driving through an uncontrolled intersection: quick to assess and ready to act. This ability makes you an outstanding decision-maker even under duress. In fact, the more pressure you are subjected to, the closer you will move toward your defaults for clean play and performance. You fully embrace the law of leadership and work to preserve your offensive advantage to be first. Your mission defensively is to "SCHOOL" your opponent and protect the "Queen" by any legal means necessary.

You are supremely confident, and your purpose and resolve is unshakable. You evoke the ire of inferior competition and the nodded respect of other true players. Purists will revel in the "basicology"™ of your play. However you must accept the reality and responsibility of continuously impacting others both positively and negatively. People's perceptions of you as a player and person will be in constant flux as they attempt to balance your ability with their ego. Still, you must continue working to minimize negative impacts involving those in your environment who cannot comprehend your prowess or processes. Your sole goal is chartable growth at all times.

Be gracious in victory and honorable in defeat. You are a Virtual artist who respects the game and others who play it. Above all, you respect yourself enough to register and accept optimization where you may find it. Grow in the game like you will play forever. Play like it is your last opportunity to perform.

About The Author

As a youngster I never quite understood when I would see a martial artist in the park going through exercises in slow motion. I thought, "He'll never fight in slow motion." Fortunately I understand now that it is less about the speed at which you train and more about the precision of technique in each frame of movement. Sustained optimization or positive repetition applied over a period of time will ultimately forge skill acquisition and prepare you for the moment of exchange. It has been a long passage thus far from Fundamentalist to "Virtualist." The road to optimization is as long as the stairway to heaven and the deeds seem just as demanding. My lifelong association with the game of basketball has given me great insight into all aspects of life. Much of who I am today is a result of my journey through the game as a fan, a student, player, and now as a coach and teacher.

I was born into basketball. As a little boy I wanted to be like my dad (Eddie Miles) and Dave (Bing). My dad, an NBA All-Star was the product of Hall of Fame high school coach A.B Calvin, a staunch fundamentalist and disciplinarian. I too was raised with the basics of the game, and believe mastery of them will always be the base for formulating consistent success in whatever discipline.

Today I run an AAU organization and train players under the umbrella of Miles Ahead Virtual Training in Seattle. The Virtual Game is a formulation of material from years of training sessions. Jordan Hamilton of Lehigh University has traveled this journey with me for almost a decade. In truth, he is the Neo of this Matrix story. He has spent countless hours developing in the virtual way. His development has been remarkable and an inspiration to those who have witnessed his transformation. Hopefully my gift back to basketball will be to continue giving to others all that I have been blessed to receive and discover on my path.

NOTES

NOTES

NOTES

NOTES

CPSIA information can be obtained
at www.ICGtesting.com
Printed in the USA
LVIW022135110612

285680LV00006B